Crossing the Med Line

Memoirs of a Psychiatric Patient

Table of Contents

Preface

Although I live very well now, mental health is something that I've had to struggle with for most of my life. During the times that were most difficult for me, I was committed to several mental health facilities and psychiatric institutions in different locations and for different durations of time. I don't think a day goes by when I don't think about these times. This period of time covers the years 1995 - 2005, when my age was 15 - 25. The following are true stories of occurrences during my time in these dismal places where according to the CDC, almost 4000 patients have died over the past 10 years. In fact, in one facility I was committed to, a man was somehow able to jump from a fifth story window while I was writing this book. My family and friends know the small amount that I've told them. The fact is that most of the conditions, practices, and incidents released here have never been discussed in any way. Not even to my family. The simple truth is, what you see when you visit, is never what you get when you stay. This is my tell-all, and I don't think I was ready to release it until now. To let go of this burden, and maybe be understood a little better. Most of these stories take place in the facility where I spent the most time, but some took place in other locations as well. The happenings and opinions expressed here come from my own experiences and are not meant to describe mental health care and facilities as a whole. I am now 38 years old and cannot confirm whether or not the conditions and practices described here remain the same today. Due to this, the names of these locations have been purposely omitted. This book is also not meant to in any way discourage those with mental illness to seek help if they need it. However, family and friends may want to research the facilities around them. There are good ones out there. This is dedicated to my friends and family who never gave up on me, my doctor who always went above and beyond to help me, my wife who continues to support me today, and to all of those who are currently locked away in these forgotten places.

"Alone in the dark with nothing but your thoughts, time can draw out like a blade." - The Shawshank Redemption

Chapter One: Committed

I hate the gowns. You know, the ones you have to change into at the doctor's office. They're so drafty in the back and I always feel like everyone is just getting a full view of my white ass. As if that's not bad enough, the stupid things tie in the back. How does that help me in any way?? Nothing I can do about it though, and as I'm told, I won't be the only one wearing one. You see, you come in wearing whatever it is you were wearing, but those clothes are taken away from you as soon as you are committed. Just like jail or prison, they are locked away in property. There is an up-side though. Unlike jail or prison, you can earn your clothes back. But like I said, they must be earned. You can hang yourself with a pair of pants easily, so I get it. But you can hang yourself just as easily with a bed sheet, or this stupid gown that actually has ties right on it! The major difference is not for your own safety, but for the safety of the other patients as well. Most likely, the clothes that you were wearing when they were grilling you to see if you were fit to be part of the general public (which you never are because Hospitals are a business like any other. There to make a profit.), have pockets. Those pockets can be used to conceal numerous objects that you can use to harm another patient (and trust me, it happens, and it happens a lot), and you are not trusted yet to hold on to those objects. So, the gown it is. However, the deal is that you have the next three days to prove that you are worthy and can be trusted to wear your own clothes. You can do this by shutting up, following orders, and staying clear of anything to do with violence. You won't ever see your shoe laces or belt again though. I mean, I guess the line has to be drawn somewhere. Hell, some patients never get their clothes back at all. Some just come in naked and don't have any clothes to begin with. In the mean-time those nice new sticky-bottom hospital socks they provide for you will have to do. Hey, since the system doesn't do all that much to help you, you may as well get something for your money.

Time to get myself up there. A nurse as well as an enormous guard accompany me on the elevator ride up to the floor (psychiatric unit) where I'll be housed for God only knows for how long. This is when I can feel my heart start beating faster. Those doors are going to open, and whatever I see when they do, is going to be where I'll be living whether I like it or not. So, "ding", they open. I couldn't really see all that much yet. There were white doors ahead of me with a small very thick window on each one. I could hear this buzzing sound as I was commanded to walk forward through them as they opened. In front of me, on the floor, was a thick red line painted that ran from one side of the hallway ahead of me to the other. This was called "the med line". It was where morning noon and night, patients would line up to receive their medication. It was also used as security for the main front desk where all of the nurses worked. Before you came up to the floor, it was drilled into your head that you would never cross this line. Not for any reason. Ever. During your time here, you could only be permitted to cross this line twice. Once you were admitted, and once when you were discharged. That's it. As I stepped over this line on my way in, I could see that this is when I actually had a little luck, if there was any luck to be had here. I had the good timing to be brought onto the floor right at dinner time. This would aid me in a couple of different ways. For starters, no matter how bad the food was here, you ate it, and all of it, because you didn't get much. It was never enough. I had always thought that a stay on a floor was quite an effective diet, since you always left weighing less than when you went it. So, everyone staying on that floor was in one place at one time. It made me feel a little bit better that I didn't have to immediately come in close contact with any other patients, since the long hall that I was now in, with patient rooms all along each side, was now empty since food was here. Another benefit was that I could use this time to scope out everyone I'd be locked up with. I could see who had a gown, who had their clothes, who seemed to be more social, who seemed like loners, who seemed angry, who seemed calm, who was old, who was young, who seemed more with it, who was just standing there scratching away at themselves, who seemed more sedated, and who seemed like they may be on a lighter medication. There seemed to be a good mix of all of this. See? Believe me, there's a whole lot to be seen in a floor cafeteria. It's the best view at the best time. Besides the simple fact that if you're on a floor and you have food, you're not leaving that food to attack anyone. That can wait till later. Food, no matter how bad, was about the most important thing here.

11   I was told to take my food tray and head into the cafeteria to eat. I wasn't exactly hungry right now, but I thought it best to just do what I was told, or at least

make it appear as though that's what I was doing. Ahead of me, to the right, was the cafeteria. I could see it through the entry way, and also through the shatter-proof glass windows that ran along it. This is how I got my good view of the patients inside. I approached the food trays. They were stacked on a wheeling metal cart that consisted of shelves, with several trays of food on them. Each food tray had a white piece of paper sticking out of it with patient names on them. Since a few food trays were still there, I could tell there were a few patients missing from the party. I found myself having always been concerned about any patient that would pass up food while given the chance to have it. Maybe they were too heavily medicated to join this most wonderful of feasts because their issues were really that bad. Or maybe they did something to warrant themselves a stay in ISO (that's isolation). As I stood by the cart searching for my food tray, I made a point to read the names of the patients who weren't present for dinner, as that information might come in useful later. Maybe I was just reading into this situation a little too much. But on a floor, the more information you have about the other patients, the safer you are, and it's a situation where you're better to be safe (as much as you can be) than sorry. Usually because sorry came with a fight and a wound. I was fortunate over the years to not end up sorry very much. But, this fortune was given to me due to an extensive education about the way things work here. Second only to having eyes in the back of your head.

Now it was time to make what seemed to be the hardest decision of the night so far. Where to sit? I looked into the room and I could see a bunch of tables that seat four people. Some patients seemed to know each other somewhat well, and I could see were in mid-conversation. Other tables were quiet. Seated there were patients that were doing little more than looking down at their trays and scooping food into their mouths.

Decisions, decisions. Do I sit at a table of patients who seemed to all be friends? I could do that, but what if they rejected me? Thinking I was just trying to be "one of them". God only knows what that rejection would consist of. I'm more than capable of taking a simple "Go away", without my ego or my feelings being harmed all that much. But what if I was met with violence, and from more than one person? My current location and state of mind required very little of what anyone thought of me. So, abandoning those tables as an option, I looked to some other ones that seemed to have a much lower level of activity. They were just about to the point of total silence. However, these seemed even worse to me. Nobody was talking to each other. Nobody even looking at each other. Other than a decision based solely on appearance, these tables were even harder to read than the others. Finally, I saw a table that was in the back corner of the cafeteria that was completely empty. So, I made the decision to sit there based completely on strategy. For one, this table was in a corner.

While sitting there, nobody would be out of my line of sight. In addition, I thought maybe it would be best for me to sit alone, and if anyone wanted to speak to me, they could do so. Instead of injecting myself into any kind of social situation that was already taking place.

So, my decision was made. I finally decided to walk towards my target. A nice blank table of solitude. I could feel my heart rate pick up again and could feel sweat on my body now as I made my way through a room of mental patients. Rounding the patients that were simply standing there scratching and talking to themselves, I made it a point to not make eye contact with anybody. Even though I could feel their eyes all over me. I could just sense it, and it seemed to raise the room temperature every second. But I just kept my eyes on the prize the whole time. Locked on to that nice empty table where I could finally just sit alone and not enjoy a single bite of my dinner. I reached my seat without incident and sat in the corner facing the crowded room. But I would still not look anyone in the eye. Feeling uncomfortable not knowing what was going on in this room, I looked up every once in a while, but only at the floor in front of me. I used my peripheral vision to sense if anyone was coming near. For the time being nobody was. So, I lifted the plastic top off of my food tray. To be honest, the food was just as I expected. But at least it wasn't worse. There was a small portion of green beans, a thin slice of what I think was chicken, covered in what I think was gravy, along with a small carton of milk. Off to the side was a plastic fork, plastic butter knife, and a small napkin. At this moment, I was actually comforted somewhat by having these things. I was sitting there, nobody was bothering me, and I could just continue to get quick snapshots of the room while I ate the food I hoped my insurance company wasn't paying too much for.

Suddenly, as I kept looking up ahead of me to the floor, I could see someone approaching me. Getting closer and closer with each glance. She was a thin frail woman who seemed to be most likely in her late 50's. I didn't look up at her. I continued to just do nothing other than sit there quietly and eat my food. However, as she got close enough, eye contact was pretty much unavoidable to anyone who had their sense of sight and cared in the slightest bit what was going on in their immediate vicinity. So, I gave in and looked at her. She was as thin as a rail, and I realized right away that she was wearing a gown. In fact, you've all seen her before. You know the woman you see sometimes while entering a grocery store? The one that slows your normally paced walk to just about a stand still as you try to reach a basket or a cart because she's just so frail and slow? Well, that's her. She had long hair down to about the middle of her back. It seemed to be wavy. Or maybe curly? Seeing as how fuzzy and dirty it was, I couldn't quite tell. It was streaked between black and a very light gray, and I actually imagined it probably looked very nice about thirty years ago. Her face was just as boney as the rest of her and looked like a windshield due to her glasses. Each lens was made of a square that must have been three inches by three inches, and she certainly had a message for me.

Here I thought to myself that maybe I had another stroke of luck. Here was the sweet old lady who was going to welcome me and tell me I was fine and had nothing to worry about. I couldn't have been more wrong. I could already see a look of anger in her eyes. She raised her arm slowly to point her finger at me. The old digit stuck out at me like an old dead stick you'd come across while hiking in the woods. Finally, she opened her mouth to speak. But she didn't just speak to me. She screamed at the top of her lungs. "What are you doing here?!" She screamed as loud as she could. I sat straight up in my chair now, for she definitely had my full attention. It would become very obvious that she actually wasn't asking my specific reason as to why I was here. What I did that landed me in this place. As my education regarding where I found myself locked away would continue, taught by these scholars of professors all around me, I'd learn that asking that specific question was frowned upon, and would start a fight half the time. You simply asked what medications they had you taking here. "Treats", they called them. Short for "treatment". Then based on the medication and what it's used to treat, you could make a guess that usually ended up to be pretty accurate. "You told President Kennedy thirty years ago that you would go out and get a job!!", this old hag continued to yell at me. This was confusing since I was only 16 years old at the time and had certainly never met President Kennedy. He had been assassinated long ago. She continued to scream nonsense that I couldn't possibly understand. So much for the sweet old lady that was just going to greet me and offer me some sort of comfort.

As I looked up at her, scared completely white I'm sure, I also made sure to look around me at the other patients. They were just continuing to eat like nothing was happening! The woman continued to scream at me with every single ounce of energy she could muster. Things that I couldn't even begin to understand. However, as she continued to scream, she also continued to take one step towards me after another. Since before this incident I could completely do without, I was trying my hardest to enjoy this so-called dinner, my arms were up on the table. Each one at the sides of my food tray. I found myself, acting upon instinct alone, slowly gripping my plastic butter knife and lowering it down to my lap underneath the table. It was almost as if I was absolutely unaware of my actions at all. I snapped the knife in two as quietly as I could. Not the way you would snap a twig in two in the woods to build a fire. I twisted the piece of plastic in my fingers. My right hand moving forward away from me, and my left hand moving towards me. The plastic snapped in two just the way I hoped it would. The large wide flat piece of the blade meant to spread condiments broke off in my right hand, while in my left hand, broke off the handle into a spiked sharp piece of plastic. Since things were certainly very tense, I put the sharp shard of plastic in my lap, and just held it there as I continued to endure this absolute nonsense spewing so loudly it hurt my ears. I thought to myself that this was some decrepit old lady, and that I didn't need a weapon at all, but my hands did what they did, almost under no control of my own.

Just as she was taking another step closer, I could see two men in white approaching her from behind. One was a big strong blonde man who looked like he could bench press 1000 pounds. The other was a black man who looked like he could bench press the white man. Each man grabbed her by the arm, one on one side, one on the other. They picked her up and began to carry her backwards away from me. This only seemed to increase her anger towards me. She kicked and fought against them and screamed at me even louder. The whole room was watching now. She kicked and screamed and fought them as hard as she could. I could see them carry and drag her back to what was the isolation room. There was a white bed in there just like you'd see in a hospital. Except on this bed, I could see large brown leather belts. There must have been three or four of them. I saw one guard wrestle her down on to the bed while the other closed the door. Later I would learn that, like I said before, this was the isolation room. Out of control patients would be taken there kicking and screaming and fighting guards. Doing what the patients referred to as "the Thorazine shuffle". Hours later they would emerge hair messed up, pupils the size of a pie, and walking with lethargy while they slurred their speech due to one or more injections of that heavily sedating drug.

So as if I'd even had an appetite before, I'd surely lost it by now. I left the cafeteria and put my tray back where I found it on the dinner cart shelf. I kept the plastic pieces of the butter knife for myself. Since each tray was named, I didn't want to put it back there for fear that they'd see it and know that I attempted to make a weapon. Again, I was probably reading into this too far, but I couldn't take any chances yet. I made my way to my assigned room. There really wasn't too much to it. Just a room with a bed. The bed was surprisingly comfortable though. I really wasn't expecting that. There was a basic bathroom. It had a toilet, sink, and unlockable wood door. I laid there on my back with many fears and many questions going through my head. There were a couple things I had to accept. One, was that I was here until they decide to let me out. No matter how bad it was, this was my home now. This is where I'd live. The other thought was something that sickened me. I had to slow my thoughts and realize that now I'm in a place where my natural instinct, without too much thought about it, without even that much time here, was to make a weapon as quickly as I could out of whatever was in arms reach. This is the thought that made me sick. This was the thought that made me realize where I am, and this is the thought that would keep me up all night. I broke the pathetic knife I made into small pieces and flushed them down the toilet, thinking it best not to keep it. As it turned out, during the loud and angry night ahead, I realized I wouldn't have gotten much sleep anyway.

Chapter Two: 501A.

       Sitting on my bed, on top of the little hospital blanket they give you in a half-ass attempt to keep you warm, I realized it was time to stop being stunned. I had to pull myself together now. Awesome or shitty (of course on the shitty side), this is where I was going to be housed. That reality is hard, especially your first time. But, it is reality none the less. So, I better start to look around and learn a little more about what's immediately around me. The bed itself was actually fairly decent. It really was better than I expected from having looked around and seen what I could see of the rest of this place. It was a basic frame with a basic twin mattress to go with it. Along the perimeter of the bed, the wood frame ran along the floor all of the way around it. They couldn't have you hiding items or God knows what underneath the bed. I stood up slowly and made my way to the window. It was actually a decent size window. I was grateful for that, as it would serve as one of my very few connections with the outside world. During the day, I could see over the rooftops of many houses, and even the very peaks of the mountains in the distance. Although I would still have to look at them through steel. It was night now though, and I could see nothing but darkness. The frame of the window was made of very thick steel. It would run about three inches wide around the whole window, and about two inches deep until it met the glass. The glass itself was very thick as well. It was shatter-proof, and it worked very well. Believe me, I've witnessed tests against it's strength. It also had steel wiring that ran through it. So, even if it was broken, the web of steel netting would remain. We called this "jump glass'. As it's intent was obviously to be a barrier against you meeting the outside world, whether it be to kill yourself or escape. The steel was, of course, very uninviting, and was also very cold. As was the glass. I'm not sure why, but it was always that way. No matter the season, or the temperature outside, it was always very cold.

On the window sill I noticed a small plastic bottle. I picked it up to see what it was. I was very much hoping that it was juice or some type of other drink I may have. Upon reading the label, I learned that it was actually mouthwash. You see, mouthwash being brought from the outside onto the floor was strictly forbidden. This is because some types of mouthwash contain alcohol. Some patients on the floor were there due to their struggles with alcoholism. In severe cases, these patients would consume the mouthwash, ingesting any tiny bit of alcohol they could. Therefore, it was their mouthwash, or none at all. I could see why most patients went along without it. To be honest, it tasted like nothing more than dirty dish water, and for all we knew, it was! The patients serving their time in this place for alcoholism or narcotics addiction were just as bad as the craziest people there.

Understandably, they were very irritable. They were also very tough to read. No matter how much time you spent secretly observing them and their behavior. Many of the fights that broke out, whether against staff or other patients, usually involved someone detoxing from alcohol, street drugs, or prescription pain killers. Their fuses were extremely short and would sometimes be lit over nothing at all. Back to my room now. Next to my bed, up against the window, was a small dresser. This wouldn't serve me well at all at this point, since I had nothing to put in it. Standing in my stupid gown, I lost myself in all of the open drawers, and was in envy of other patients who had dressers that were full. I imagined that if I were to receive clothing, what items I would put in these drawers and where. Oh well. Maybe someday soon. Other than the small bed, and the small dresser that was next to it, these was nothing else in the room at all. My attention then turned towards the bathroom that was part of my room. I could see the door was open a bit, and the small light-green tiles that made up the floor. I then went to investigate it. I pushed the door open and could see that it was very small. At this point, I didn't care about it's size. I was actually just happy to have a bathroom of my own. It was no more than a 5x4 space with a toilet, a sink, and a mirror. Of course, the mirror wasn't glass. That would never have endured here for very long. It was simply a highly polished piece of metal bolted to the wall. But at least it was enough to get a basic image of your current self in between the scratches and worn areas from the many patients that were there before you.

What you would not find here was a toothbrush, shaving razor (obviously), or shower. A toothbrush was later brought to me as a favor from my mother. After her gifts to me were fully inspected before they'd cross the med line. Since I did not find the mouthwash to be of any use at all, I emptied it's contents down the sink, threw away the cap, and used the bottle as a toothbrush holder that would stay on top of my sink. It worked quite nicely. A shaving razor is very understandably missing. There is not the slightest chance in hell you would be handed a razor here, and with good reason. Considering the violent, suicidal, and self-mutilators that inhabited this place. If you wanted to shave, you must ask permission from the guards. Once permitted, two guards would accompany you to your room. Once there, they would hand you a bottle of shaving cream. One guard would stand on one side of you, and another on the other side of you as they allowed you to lather the cream on your face. Then you would hand the bottle back to them when you were ready to proceed and shave. One of the guards would then ask you which hand you preferred to hold a shaving razor in. Next, one guard would hand you a disposable razor in your preferred hand, while the other guard would hold you by your other wrist. Of course, this was an attempt to keep you from harming either yourself, or them. You would have one hand free with your shaving razor for the remainder of your shave. I understood the precaution, and I'm sure it was quite normal to them given their profession. But to me it was still very awkward. I understood their position completely but couldn't help but feel embarrassed as they very closely watched my every move as I went about what used to be a normal part of my every morning. This was actually the reason I started wearing facial hair to this very day. It was much more uneventful. If you kept an electric shaver or trimmer locked up in your property, and showed you could be trusted to use it, they would usually provide it for you upon request. Then you could go to your room and use it by yourself for a period of ten minutes, since it was much harder to harm yourself with one of these types of grooming products.

Taking a shower worked in a similar sort of way. Just like shaving, you would request permission from the guards to take a shower. As long as you haven't given them any trouble recently, and they had a few free minutes, permission would be granted. After all, they didn't want you to stink any more than you did. Also, lice and other types of infections would cause a problem on the floor from time to time. It never really imposed a huge threat but was never surprising either. So even if you were denied a shower at the time that you requested one, chances were very good that you would still be allowed to take one at some point that day. That is why you learned not to request a shower late in the day. The earlier in the day you requested a shower, the better your chances were that day of receiving one. Once permission was granted, you were given two towels. You would then go to your room, undress, and wrap one towel around your shoulders and upper body, and wrap the other around your waist and lower body. That rule was the same for both men and women. You must remember that some patients are here for different types of sex addiction disorders, and you must cover yourself as much as possible. This rule was the same for clothing as well. Once you proved yourself worthy of wearing your own clothes, it would be at the discretion of the staff. Once you returned to the hallway shower door covered in your towels, one of the guards would thoroughly pat you down for any objects that you might use to harm yourself, or them. Once your inspection was complete, you would have five minutes, and not one second longer to take a shower. When I say five minutes, I mean five minutes. Exactly at that time, if you haven't completed your shower, the guard would open the shower door and shut the water off whether you were finished or not, and whether you were completely naked or not. Again, I guess I somewhat understood these precautions. They didn't apply so much to me, but I knew the patients they had to deal with. The shower itself seemed smaller than a phone booth. It was like stepping into a small locker. It had no shelves, and just a basic shower head, knobs, and a drain on the floor. The hospital was large, and I'm sure the pipes were very old. So, it would take a good couple of minutes for the water to come up to a comfortable temperature. Although it would eventually do this, it shaved minutes off of your already short amount of time. Eventually I learned to open the shower door after I was searched, turn the shower on, and stand outside of it and feel the water. I would wait and do this until the water temperature came up to one that was comfortable. Then I would step in and close the door, making the most out of the five minutes I was allowed.

Chapter Three: Lights Out

Now that the inspection of my room was complete, I wondered to myself, what do I do next? I wasn't familiar with this place enough to just leave what had now become my best comfort of all, my new room. This place was a new fortress of solitude to me now, and I certainly had no plans of leaving it any time soon. How lucky I thought I was to score one of only two single-bed rooms. One was in my wing, wing A, and the other in wing B. I thought maybe if I left my room I could explore a little more. However, I knew that meant possibly coming face to face with other patients. At this point, I did not entertain this thought one bit. After all, I was only on this floor for a few minutes before I was screamed at by some lunatic who I immediately then after saw dragged away, doing "the Thorazine shuffle", as we called it. I didn't want to know anybody here. I was frightened, cold, and alone. As far as I knew, everybody outside my door was an enemy. I had my own issues to work on here. On top of that, I was just being pissed off. It was about 7 or 8 pm now, so I decided to just lay on my bed and try my best to just relax and try to let the reality that I'm locked in this place sink in a little more. I had to try my best to accept it. I knew that once I got myself beyond that, I could get my wits back as to what's going on around me and defend myself better.

I laid on my back on my little bed with my stupid gown on. From the location of my room I could hear many things. My room being 501A, the first room down that long hallway, was closest to "the hive". That's what we called the nurses' station. It got it's name from it's round shape and the fact that several workers were always going in and out of it. It was the same for the first room along wing B. It was a single-bed room closest to the hive. Behind the hive was a large thick wooden door that had the same steel frame around it that the windows had. We called that room "the drug den". It was simply the pharmacy for the floor. Where all types of medications for the patients were stored. Being in room 501A had it's advantages. First of all, as mentioned before, it was a single-bed room. Nothing to have to share, and no crazy person right in there with me. Also, I could get a kind of "first scoop" on what was going down on the floor. I could hear which staff member was going to work which hours, what was happening with what patient, conversations between patients on the med line and staff, when new patients were coming up to the floor and why, what room they'd be going into, and so on. As with any jail or prison, patients would barter and trade with each other for all types of things. Whether it be for a book, a pair of headphones, food, sharps items, cell phones, socks, smokes, damn near anything you could think of. And these were the items they'd use to make the trades, along with pain killers and other medications. It was mostly the younger patients that took part in this. I guess trades for me could've come when someone new was coming to the floor, since I usually knew everything about it. Some patients would often ask me during breakfast if anybody new was coming to the floor, and if I knew anything about them, but I wasn't really interested in any kinds of trades. I think this gained me some favor with the other patients. Since I wasn't interested in any forms of currency they used, I guess a little information was traded for a little bit of appreciation and respect. Respect was a huge deal here amongst those here for criminal actions but who were sent to a floor due to whatever diagnosis they had, instead of going to jail. Fortunately, I wasn't really a part of that. But for them, respect was demanded. But as long as it was given, it was almost always received. However, if it wasn't, it was almost always grounds for a fight. Fights were common due to the circumstances of where we were. We were all labeled insane! Therefore, there were no legal consequences. A fight in jail can bring you more charges. Not in here though. One time I even saw a guy get stabbed in the back with a fork, which then led to a bad fight. But this would basically get you shit on by the guards, and being on their nice list was very important to me as it just made life a little easier. This was only a big problem in one facility where I stayed. Different floors had different expectations of what you would do when any violence broke out. In some facilities, you were required to go to your room and shut the door. This way, the guards had plenty of room to do what they needed to in order to gain control over those in a fight. Also, you were moved to a safe location. Other facilities simply demanded that if you were not involved, you would get down on your knees with your hands on your head. Another one of the advantages of room 501A is that I enjoyed most was that, other than activity from the hive, there was hardly any traffic going back and forth past my doorway since it was at the beginning-end of the hall. Like I said, information on new patients was very important. Not to mention, there was of course a general curiosity. Whenever you are new to a floor, as other patients walk by your doorway, they will always stroll more slowly by, looking in your bedroom at you the whole time. Just to learn anything about you that they could. I'm guilty of having done it myself. Since this was my first stay on a floor, I made the rookie mistake of acting the way that I did. Not talking to anyone and isolating myself in my room for the entire rest of the night. This was a red flag showing that I have never been on a floor before, and that perhaps I could be taken advantage of. I would later learn that it's best to act at home right off the bat. Talk to people, don't act nervous, and maybe speak some lingo that we use here.

"Lights out!! Silence!!" Those orders were barked very loudly by a guard exactly at 10 pm every night. There were of course a couple minutes of noises being made by patients rushing to their rooms, putting things away, and getting ready for bed before they turned out their lights. I turned my bedroom light out and crawled into my bed. I pulled the covers high up over me due to the cold, and just laid there still. I wanted to fall asleep. I knew already that sleep would be important here. But I couldn't fall asleep. I just laid there, eyes open, just listening and thinking. Try as you may before these commands were given, this is when it really hits home. Where you were, where you would be when you wake up, and where you will still be staying beyond that. I have seen and heard first timers go ballistic at this point. Screaming that they want their family, their spouse, that it was a mistake that they're here, or simply that the staff better let them out "or else". All soon to be dragged away doing the Thorazine shuffle. As for myself, I remained as silent as I could. Laying on my pillow and gripping my blanket tight. I was more of a thinker I guess. I thought of home and of my family. I wondered what my friends and my siblings were doing right now. Just hanging out and watching TV. Or maybe out at the mall. I wondered how my mother was, and if she was thinking of me as well. I wondered what it was like with my seat at the dinner table empty, and what it was my mother made for dinner. How long would it be before I could taste one of her home cooked meals again? I had to fight off thoughts of her oven cooked chicken because if I thought hard enough, I could both smell and taste it. Right along with her kielbasa and fried potato perogies. My mother was off-the-boat Polish and believe me, she could cook! I had to shut thoughts of all these things out though, as well as what my family and friends might be doing. Thoughts of home, family and friends could bring just as much pain as they could bring comfort. I had to focus on myself and where I was now. I needed to remain calm. After all, the night was extremely young, and I was soon to learn that many things went "bump" in the night here.

Alone, quiet and cold, I laid there in my bed. Some low light from the hallway keeping me from complete darkness. Most patients knew the drill. Remain silent and you won't get hollered at or dragged off to isolation. These were the people who still had a little more to their minds left, or who weren't so drugged up that they were half asleep and drooling on themselves anyway. This is when I found out the cons to being in my specific room. The first and most annoying thing came right away from the hive. The doors to this place were kept locked by a steel bolt that was electronically controlled by the nurses working behind the hive. Any time a nurse, doctor, or anyone else who had access to the floor wanted in, there would be a loud buzzing noise followed by a deep thump. I remembered these sounds from when I was first brought up here. The hive was only a few feet from the locked doors with jump glass windows on them. Whenever someone wanted access, they would knock on the door, show themselves in the window, and press their ID badge against it. The nurse in the hive, then recognizing this person had access to the floor, would then hold down a button that electronically controlled the door lock. This would create the loud buzzing sound, followed by the thump of the bolt that locked the door sliding out of the way, and granting this person access to the floor. The loud buzzing sound would remain constant until the doors closed behind them, and the loud thump of the bolt sliding back into place was complete. This seemed to go on constantly until around midnight or 1 am when shift changes between nurses and staff were complete. Even if you did manage to fall asleep in between their comings and goings, the activation of the main door was sure to wake you soon. These main doors were labeled by the patients "the slammer", and rightfully so. It was during the nights here that I soon began to wonder if my room was the best room, or the worst room.

At first, despite this constant banging, I did manage to get a half hour to an hour of sleep here and there. In between the slammer doing it's thing to keep the general public safe from us crazies. There was also the hourly "beaming". Beaming was another precaution that the hospital took. I understood this one as well, but it still could be a nuisance. A nurse that worked the night shift would be given a flashlight and a clip board. Then once every hour she would make her rounds. Opening your door, flashing her light in "beaming" you, and marking down in her records that you were still present. For example, we would ask "Who's beaming tonight?" Again, an understandable precaution I guess, and usually if I did manage to get some sleep, I was rarely woken by a simple beaming. I would also come to learn that it really was necessary. Over my years I have seen several escape attempts. None of them were successful. Some beamers were better than others, which is why other patients would usually ask me before lights out who was on duty that night. When it came to patients and their precious sleep, there was a preferred and non-preferred way of going about this task. The preferred way was to open the door quietly, shine the flashlight on the floor, and then use it's soft reflection to mark the patient as present. This was a floor, so they used some pretty damn powerful flashlights. The non-preferred way was to open the door however you wanted, shine the light directly on the patient's face, and then walk away leaving the door wide open. To you the reader, this might not seem like a big deal. But you must remember where we are. Of course, sleep was very important, but it was also just a matter of principal and dignity. We deserved some common courtesy. Those that beamed us in the face didn't care about us. Instead of viewing us as decent people and patients in a facility for some help, these nurses viewed us as less than human, and simply didn't care. To us, it just made us feel like prisoners who deserved to be where we are. It was simply a matter of disrespect and principal. As for my sleep, it would only come during the first few hours of my nights in 501A. After that, every night seemed to be fight night. I don't know if night time medications wore off, or those who couldn't sleep just got bored, or if those withdrawing just couldn't keep still and became angry, but sure enough, the screaming would come. I often pitied the beaming night nurse. Those who couldn't sleep often became enraged at her. I understood that it didn't help, but you're on a floor, not in a Hilton. And most likely, that's not what was causing your inability to sleep anyway. I guess some patients just wanted somebody to take their anger out on. Some would just scream at her. Others would make such an issue out of it that it would turn into a physical fight. Also, after lights out, you were not supposed to leave your room at all unless you had some sort of immediate need. Yet some patients would wonder down the hall at night. Slowly strolling as if they didn't have a care at all, and weren't aware of this very strict rule. Again, some would get angry and scream as the guards demanded that they return to their room, and others would find it necessary to come to blows over this. Some patients were just batshit crazy and that's all there was to it. Laying in their beds, they would scream all kinds of nonsense that you couldn't understand, and then fight the guards when they simply came to help them.

The problem for me came when it was time to finally restrain these patients. One after another they were brought passed my door on their way to isolation. Doing the Thorazine shuffle as they seemed to be fighting the guards for their lives. Kicking, screaming, and doing anything they could in an attempt to break free. However, freedom would never come for any of them. What did happen is that I would find out the worst problem of being stuck in room 501A. You see, being closest to the hive, room 501A shared a wall with isolation. As I laid in my bed, after the big show had passed by my doorway (even though I tried not to look), I could still hear everything that went on in the next room. The screaming would continue, and the fighting would continue. About every five seconds someone, whether it be patient or staff, was banging off the other side of my wall. This carried on night after night after night after night. The lack of sleep drained me both mentally and physically. I began to feel physically ill. I felt like I was turning onto a zombie! I had to do something. I just had to. I guess I could've complained to the guards, but I was new here. I didn't want to make any waves. Especially since their first impressions of me seemed to be good. As good as you could get in here anyway. Also, would they really move me to another room, which might not even be available, just because I couldn't get any sleep? I hardly thought so. So, I finally came up with a plan. One night, as all the screaming and fights began, I got out of my bed and gathered up all of my blankets and my pillow. I brought them all into the bathroom and shut the door behind me. At this point, I didn't care what the night nurse thought. I'd do anything for just a few straight hours of sleep. I spread my blankets and my pillow out on the tile floor so that my feet would be down by the toilet, and my head against the opposite wall. I turned the light off, and laid down in my new cold, hard, small bedroom. I found this to be incredibly sad, but I just couldn't take any more sleep deprivation. Otherwise I'd end up like one of these crazies myself! It seemed to help at first. It muffled the screams and the banging against my wall. However, I could still hear it all. It still kept me awake. That's when I got the idea to try and use the bathroom fan. I reached up and turned the fan switch on. Immediately I could hear it turn on, and even better, drown out the noise of anything else that was going on. I was finally able to sleep! The night nurse didn't wake me, nor did anyone else. I imagined I slept pretty deeply. I could only assume that they knew why I was sleeping where I was, and just let it go. So, there I was. Sleeping on the small, cold, hard floor of the bathroom in room 501A. Letting the drone of the fan protect my slumber. Was this the best room? The worst room? Really, the answer was neither. Everything beneficial here came with a price, and one way or another, you paid it.

The morning was a rude awakening. I imagine it had to be better for others than it was for me, and I was correct. On a normal morning, anywhere between 7:30 and 8:00 am, the guard would open your door and loudly yell "breakfast!!" You were then expected to get up at once, come out of your room, and grab your food tray on the way to the cafeteria. Still groggy from either medication or lack of sleep, you would sit there and use your plastic fork to shovel breakfast into your mouth. Too tired to even care what it was. Usually it was powder eggs, two slices of toast, and a small carton of milk. Breakfast never fully satisfied your hunger and was probably the smallest meal we were given. Some patients, including myself, were not allowed to have any caffeine in their diet at all due the fact that it may interact with medications, or worsen certain psychiatric conditions. This didn't help to move your morning along either. It was very frowned upon by both the staff and the guards to not get up and grab your tray from the food cart racks when you were told to. I can assume just because you simply weren't following orders. Some patients, usually the ones on high doses of stronger medications, or that have done the Thorazine shuffle overnight, just weren't able to get up at that time in the morning. Even after they've been yelled at for a second time. Personally, I preferred it that way. If your status with the guards was pretty good, then you could grab the tray of a missing patient and have it for yourself. I never kept it to myself though. I always asked who wanted what from the tray. After calling what was mine of course. You never took their tray too soon though. You had to finish your breakfast first. Then, once you were done, and a time had passed that made it clear that these patients wouldn't be joining us, then you could go ahead and grab it without anyone really saying anything. That's why breakfast was my most favorite meal of all here. Even though what they served you was small, breakfast was the meal when most patients were missing.

Therefore, this is when you definitely got the most food. These mornings were the norm, but the first few were different for me. When I was committed, I was told that a nurse would be coming to my room every morning at 6:00 am to draw my blood so that they could monitor my Tylenol and opiate levels until they were considered to be nontoxic. I was told very firmly that these mornings would go "without incident or any trouble from me". I remember how much I would've loved to tell them that if they wanted something to go without incident, then don't shake me awake at 6:00 am to take my blood. But I certainly had no authority here in the least bit. Also, I knew the blood had to be collected before I ate anything, and also my wellbeing. In addition to that, I also had to accept the consequences for my own actions. So that's how it was. Every morning at 6:00 am a nurse would come into my room toting her little kit for collecting blood samples. Sometimes I would already be awake, and it wasn't really that bad. Other times I was shaken awake, and before I even knew it, a needle was shoved into my arm. After about five mornings waking up to that, they stopped coming because my levels had dropped to a normal level. My arm remained sore for a while after they stopped collecting blood due to the fact that they did not alternate which arm they were taking blood from each morning. After that, when the guards barked their morning orders, I simply got up and followed them.

Chapter Four: Passing Time

When I think back on my time on floor, I remember the very first thing that made me smile. I finally got my clothes! I don't even really know who gave them back to me. I woke up in the morning of my fourth day, after proving myself during my first three days of being worthy enough to receive them, and they were just in a neat pile on my nightstand. It was only one pair, the pair I came in with, but I didn't care about that at all for now. I was finally done with my crappy gown! I had socks, a pair of jeans, a tee shirt, hoodie, and pair of shoes. Of course, no shoe laces or a belt though. I didn't mind that either. It was already explained that these wouldn't be allowed. So, the tongue of everyone's shoes hung out and as their soles dragged on the floor when they walked. This is why I actually didn't bother to wear my shoes all that much. Without the laces they were sort of floppy and uncomfortable. I just stuck to those hospital socks with the grippy little soles. I saw that the string of my hoodie was cut out as well. At the age of 38 I still to this day cut the string out of any hoodie I buy. I wore my hoodie so much that way on the floor that it just became what I was used to. I gave the staff permission ahead of time to do that should I earn my clothes back. Having clothes was great. You just didn't look as crazy anymore. Finally, I wasn't so cold anymore! I wore my hoodie basically nonstop due to how cold the floor always was. One of the best benefits of having your clothes back was that you didn't look like a newbie anymore. New patients that joined our crap hole here would see me and not be able to tell whether I was there for three days or three months. "Frequent Flyers", as we called them, to floors wouldn't be able to tell whether this was my first rodeo or not. A simple benefit, but still a benefit. Not only that, but my room was moved to one more towards the middle of the hall. Sleep was much easier this way, and I began to feel much more rested. I also felt a little better about leaving my room.

Now that I started leaving my room more, I found what came to be my most beloved thing of all here, and I can still see it so vividly in my mind. One morning, after I had finished my breakfast in solitude, sporting my new outfit and glancing up from time to time to watch the room, I placed my tray back on the food cart when I saw it. As I turned around, about to head back to my room, there it was. The biggest, brightest, clearest window I had ever seen. How could I have missed it before?? I guess I was just too caught up in trying to adapt to my surroundings. It was at the end of the hall of my wing, which probably ran about 75 yards long, with bedroom doors lining each side. It literally captivated me. I stared at it as if it were the only thing here. Nothing broke my gaze as my legs started walking my body towards it, almost completely under control and acting with no effort from me. I passed by patient's bedrooms and some of them in the hallway as if they weren't even there, finally reaching my glorious destination. The window was about six feet wide and six feet high. But in this moment, to me, it could've covered a square mile. I didn't even notice what was outside it, as I couldn't help but look at the window itself first. It had the same steel frame that ran around all of the other windows here. There was about a twelve inch shelf on the bottom of it. But what made me notice it in the first place, and why it looked so beautiful, was that it was the only window on the floor that didn't have the steel netting throughout the glass. I hadn't seen that in a while, and it was gorgeous to me. I guess they got away with it because the glass looked to be about a half inch thick. I remember thinking that maybe it was bullet proof. I also noticed, that even here in this place, it had not one fingerprint on it. Not a single smudge, and not a single spot. The entire thing was crystal clear. Outside I could see all kinds of things. The many things that exist in a normal world. The sky was clear blue. Without a single cloud and the sun was shining bright. I could see the streets, cars, people walking on the sidewalks having no idea I was here watching them, houses, trees, grass. If it was quiet enough I could slightly hear the sounds of the busy outside world, but that didn't happen too often. Right in front of me on the ground was the emergency parking lot. Just to the right, the emergency room with it's big lit up sign and large automatic main doors. I could see an ambulance parked there as well. This was so great! I could watch ER patients come and go, watch the ambulances with their bright lights, even guess what was wrong with the poor people they delivered. An amazing way to pass some time, I thought.

"That there's the wishing window". I heard a voice say behind me. I turned around quickly with an initial feeling of fear. God only knows who it was. As it turned out, it was just another patient. He was a tall guy. A bit scruffy, but about as clean cut as you around here. Probably a couple years older than me. Short dark hair with a short beard, and just wearing jeans and a dark sweater. I eased up somewhat, seeing his calm demeanor and noticing his hands were in his pockets. This was the first patient to speak to me, so I was a little surprised and kind of at a loss for words. He approached the window very similar to the way I did before stopping next to me. Smiling and looking out it like he was beholding the greatest thing ever. "Awesome ain't it?" He continued. I still found myself not really sure about what to say. Could I actually just have a conversation here? Are there patients that were capable of this simple action? "The wishing window?" I managed to finally speak out. "Yeah." He replied. "You know. So you can wish you were one of them people out there instead of stuck in here with us crazies." "Oh. I get it." I replied nodding. "Just don't touch it." He instructed. I would come to learn that the wishing window was loved by all patients. Leaving just a single fingerprint on it was not only disrespectful to all of them, but also to the window itself. As if it were some sort of prized possessions to all of us imprisoned here. It was important that it remain spotless so that all could enjoy it. Also, it would come to be known as a safe place to meet whenever any patients wanted to discuss something serious. As it was the farthest location from the hive. Usually if there were two people there, you let them finish their business before approaching. "Sure thing." I said. "I'll remember that." "I'm Dave." He said. "I'd shake your hand but.. You know." His head making a motion toward the hive. Physical contact between patients was strictly forbidden here. I nodded to him. "Scott." I replied. Dave respectfully nodded back. "Look at that boy yonder." Said Dave. Half excited and pointing out the window. "That boy done busted his leg." I looked out the window at what seemed to be two parents helping their son as he hobbled toward the emergency door. "For sure it be that leg. You know it cause he still got both shoes on. If it be his ankle they take that shoe off. Then it hurts worse than a kick in the nuts to put it back on. So they just go on doin' without it. At least he'll be sleepin' in his own bed tonight. Even be it hardly nothin' for comfort." "He sure is lucky I guess." I said, sadly agreeing that a broken leg was better than being here.

"I know why you're here. If that's ok to say." Dave said. Lowering his voice a little. Maybe as not to upset me. "It's ok. I be here for the same thing." He continued. Puzzled, I asked the question, "How do you know?" "I seen your sitter come up with you." He replied. You see, if you're in the ER or just taken to the hospital while they're waiting for a floor room to become available, you get a "sitter". This is a nurse who would take a seat in a chair next to your bed and sit there all night while you slept. Making sure you did nothing crazy or hurtful throughout the night. It's definitely pretty awkward. They just sit there all night and watch you sleep. Sometimes they'll talk with you, but most times they're completely silent. "Oh." I replied. Looking out the wishing window. I'm sure a little embarrassed at the time. "Don't worry. Things will get better for you here." Dave reassured me. Folding his arms as he continued to stare out the wishing window. He then said to me, "The biggest question of all be, if the slammer were done stuck wide open right now, would you leave?" The first thought that jumped in my mind was, "Hell yes!" "For me", Dave continued, "they could take the slammer right off the hinges. Don't make no difference. I'd still be sleepin' here tonight. I guess I just ain't ready." Dave said as he looked at the floor. "You gotta ask yourself that question. Are they really keeping you here, or do you be knowin' you belong here? That question could be changin' a whole lot." Dave said as he looked back out the wishing window. "Well, I'll leave you to it." Said Dave, as he strolled away. Dave had a point. What if I returned home right now? After everything I've been through just a few days ago. Sitting there alone in the dark. Not much to do except think. Would I bring myself to the edge of sanity, just winding up here again anyway? Would I completely be safe in a world where I had access to anything I wanted, instead of here where I was kept safe from others, as well as myself? To be honest, I wasn't sure of the correct answer. Dave had dropped quite a bomb on me, and just gave me the best advice I've ever been given on a floor. I understood immediately why he said what he did. If you were here by choice, then that overcame everything else here. It made every horrible thing less horrible. For no matter what or who it was you encountered here, you knew it was better for you to be here than on the "outside." You were here by choice, instead of being imprisoned. This, even if only slightly, improved your morale. Although, honestly, Dave spoke as though he had never completed the third grade, I quickly realized how smart he actually was. I liked him immediately, and knew we'd become friends. Also, his knowledge of this place and his attention to detail was very important to me. I knew he was someone I could trust in this place. For now, I stood here with my new best friend, and what would come to be the thing I spent more time with than anybody else here. This window.

As several more days went on, I eventually started a basic friendship with a few other patients. Dave and I seemed to be the tightest. Soon I met Amanda. She was a short little blonde girl. Fair skinned with dark brown eyes. She was very nice, and most often was smiling. However, she was not somebody who you wanted to make angry, as she had a bad temper and a short fuse. She also had a tendency to not be able to sit in one place for very long. She often stood instead of sitting, pacing from one place to another. I never asked her about it (I never liked to ask anyone), but for these reasons I assumed she was there for some type of bipolar disorder. Other than that, she seemed to have her wits about her. Then there was Mike. He was the funny one. Sort of the class clown type. We enjoyed being around him, as he could somehow always find a way to make us laugh. He had a couple of buck teeth, a gut he couldn't care less about, and big moon-boot white high tops that flopped along the floor as he walked. Which he also didn't care about. We all liked Mike. His personality made it most difficult to be upset with him for any reason. Flat out, he just didn't give a fuck about much. Mike was "doing time", as we'd say, to gather himself together and do the twelve-step program after just having detoxed in rehab for alcoholism. He was open about this, and although it's always tough to let your guard down, none of us considered him to be dangerous. We were not afraid around him. Becky was the next person to sort of morph into our little group. She might have been a couple of years younger than us. She was kind of a punk chick. She wore "skater" clothes, had a green streak dyed in her shoulder-length brown hair, and I could see small holes in her lip as well as her nose where she'd had piercings. The jewelry itself was missing because it was not allowed here. If you got in a fight, ripping these things out was a quick and easy way to cause an injury.

Becky had a calm way about her and a slow smile. She was a gentile and calming person who made herself easy to be around. "What's uppppppppppp." She'd say when she saw you. Always "Later!". When she left. She was here for a schizophrenic disorder. This made her interesting, as most patients being treated for this are either extremely drugged up, or just (I'm sorry to say) way too annoying to be around. If they find themselves in here anyway. She was alright though, and we all felt some sort of responsibility to keep her this way and make sure she was doing ok. I guess we felt compelled due to her diagnosis and the fact that she was the youngest of our little click. The hardest friend to make of all was Paula. Or maybe I should, it was hardest for Paula to make friends. I saw her in our little cafeteria a lot. She was always alone. Forgive me for saying, but she had the usual characteristics of a Hispanic girl. She was a little shorter, had shoulder-length dark curly hair, dark eyes, and tan skin. I'd later learn she was here for depression and suicide. At least she did have some normal visitors. It looked to be a mother and a sister. That's when I found out why she hadn't talked to anyone yet. She couldn't speak any English. Only Spanish. So, one day I had an idea. One of my favorite bands at the time was a Hispanic hardcore band out of LA called Downset. The last song on their album was all In Spanish. I took a few years of Spanish in high school, so I could speak the very basics of the language. So, I asked for my CD player out of property, and was given a 30-minute limit for it. I approached her slowly, as to not frighten her, and said hello. She said hello to me in return. I handed her the headphones and simply told her that I couldn't understand this song. She took them slowly, and put them on, I think just happy to have some sort of interaction with anyone at all. After she put them on, I pressed play, beginning the track all in Spanish. She lit up instantly. Her eyes and her smile showed just how happy she was not to be in exile anymore. From that moment on, that was it. Paula was one of us. She sat with us during meal times and could at least say hello to us, and we could say hello back. She was always happy to see us, and we were always happy to see her. She simply wasn't alone anymore. If Mike would crack a joke, and everybody laughed, I could do my best to explain it to her, and she would be able to join in the laughter as well. Honestly, I felt good about what we had done here. Who knows what Paula's time here would've been like, and how successful her recovery would've been. So here we were. Five misfits out of about 30 total patients on the floor who managed to come together to keep ourselves from going even more crazy than we already were.

Eventually, once the five of us had proven once again that we could be trusted by the staff, we were able to play some basic card and dice games. It was a great way to pass some time here, and maybe keep your attention from things going on around you. If we asked nice enough, a nurse would unlock a cabinet in the cafeteria that held pens, pencils, markers, children's scissors (since they had the plastic guard on them) and the cards and dice. The nurse would give us one pen. This pen was strictly only to be used by us and must be returned to her when we were finished. A pen wouldn't really be my first choice for a weapon. However, on another floor I saw a guy get stabbed in the back with a fork, so I guess you're better safe than sorry. We all made sure to thank the nurse very much. One game we liked to play a lot was poker. The game was short enough that we could stop it at any time if need be. However, we didn't have any chips, and we certainly didn't have any money. So, we would tear strips of paper into about the size of a dollar bill. Then we'd write a large number on each piece of paper representing the denomination and would split the "money" evenly amongst us. Then we'd play poker as if all of us were rich! Fortunately, Paula was familiar with the game and also with American currency, so she was ready to play right from the start. Dave and Mike would even make friendly bets between the two of them for cigarettes, since they both smoked the same brand. Our favorite game to play was Yahtzee. We could play that game for hours. Paula hadn't played this game before. Luckily, I could count in Spanish. When her turn came, I would play for her. Doing the best I could to count the dice up, show her how she should play this roll and why, and then mark her score card. Paula was smart though, and a quick learner. So, it didn't take more than a couple of games before she understood it and could play it just as good as the rest of us. Not to mention that after a little while of being friends with us, she had picked up some very basic English words. Of course, we made sure she knew all curse words, and would laugh with her when she used them. We were not able to yell "Yahtzee!" should any of us be lucky enough to get one though, since you weren't supposed to raise your voice here. Sometimes one of us would let it slip though, and we'd catch a scowling look from either the hive or the guards. Then we'd all look at each other, red-faced and doing our best not to laugh. The only bad part of game time is that many times it was interrupted by a fight. Whether it be between two patients, or between a patient and a guard. Since we were at the table playing a game, it was just too hard for us to get up quick enough and go to our rooms and close our doors as this floor required. Fortunately, the guards seemed to understand this, and rarely said anything to us. Instead, whoever had the pen would pocket it, and we'd all keep our hands in the air and remain still. We'd stay like that until the matter was completely resolved. I think the people that started the fight were either just bored, maybe envious that we had friends, or just the usual crazies. We had to play in the cafeteria due to the fact that there were no other tables anywhere and entering another patient's room was forbidden. The table we played at was against the left wall. Those of us who had their back to the room would often take an indirect blow from the fight going on. One time, Mike was even sucker punched from another patient from behind for no reason at all! Because of this, I always tried to get to the cafeteria as soon as I could. This way I could take a seat with a wall behind me, or a corner seat if we were going to sit at another table.

Another way to pass the time was by watching TV. We were very grateful for a TV, as most floors didn't have one. Even though it was a piece of shit kept behind a thick piece of glass, we loved it. Sometimes it would cause arguments between patients as to what to watch. If the argument was bad enough, the staff would turn the TV off. This didn't happen too often though. People knew they would catch hell from the rest of us if they were the reason why we were denied our precious TV. Also, as it turned out, Amanda was a die-hard Yankees fan. She made it known ahead of time, and very clear, that if a Yankees game was on TV that's what we'd be watching. She absolutely had to watch their games. Nobody really minded though. We were just happy to have something to watch at all, and it was just easier to go along with whatever Amanda wanted rather than face her tiny wrath. Most of us didn't care about the Yankees, or even about baseball in general. However, it was something to do, and it was even more fun to cheer them on with her and get wrapped up in it. Sometimes we would get a movie too. We would beg and beg a nurse until she finally broke down and said she would bring in a movie for us to watch. Again, we didn't even care what it was. The nurses were even kind enough to allow us to stay up an extra hour after lights out if we were watching a movie. It was like our own slumber party, and maybe even made us forget that we were here. Even if it was only for a minute.

The best passing of time of all was visiting hour. Seeing my mother and the rest of my family, if only for a little while, was definitely the thing that got me through each day the most. My sister came a lot too. They didn't come every day, but almost every day.

Any time they could. My brother lived far away during most of this period in my life, but he would still call me on the pay phone all the time. Attached to the wall down the patient hallway was the phone. Sometimes it would be hard to talk because the phone was only allowed to be used for a short period of time, and there was no shortage of patients who wanted to use it. Starting somewhere in the middle of the day, if I knew my family was coming that day, I'd watch the clock and become more and more excited. Visiting hour came before dinner time. Everyone who had a visitor would be called to the front of the floor by the hive. Of course, not beyond the med line though. We could see our visitors but couldn't reach them yet. As before our visits began, the staff would have to make sure their visit was permitted by the patient. Then the nurse would write their name down as well as who they were visiting in their log. When your time first began on the floor, you'd be given a visitor name sheet. You simply write down the names of anyone you'll allow to visit you. I would always write my family members only. I knew how much they'd want to see me. I never wrote any of my friends down though. I didn't really want them to see me in these places. I knew my family wouldn't judge me though. They've helped me through and knew about most of my problems. Although I didn't really want them to see me like this either, I could never say no to their visits. It was wonderful to see them. These were the people that I knew genuinely cared about me the most. Also, as strange as this may sound, it brought some sense of normalcy to the floor. Here were all the people from the outside. My family, my friends had their families these also. Everyone who had a visitor was happy, and sometimes they even got to meet each other. Another great thing about visits is that your family can bring things in for you. It could be toiletries, food, clothes, all kinds of items. All the items had to be checked by the staff first. Anything that could be harmful was rejected. I was most excited to have more clothes. I was wearing the only pair of clothes that I had. So even though I had the little dresser in my room, it was still empty. Having clothes to put away made me feel better, more taken care of, and even a little more normal. Another good thing about visiting hour was that it was so very stressed to us that we would be on our best behavior. So, nothing really bad ever happened. Visiting hour always went too fast though. We'd say our goodbyes and then all of the visitors were checked out. We would stand by the med line and smile and wave at them until the main doors buzzed, and it was time for them to leave. I'd stay until the slammer closed, and it's strong bolt locked back into place. At least now I would feel a little bit better about eating what they called dinner.

Chapter Five: Smokes

One "luxury" that I never thought I'd have was a smoke break. Especially because I don't smoke. Unfortunately for some, smoke breaks are a thing of the past. Due to new regulations, hospitals, as well as their grounds, are now completely tobacco free. If you come on to a floor now and you're a smoker, you have two choices as to how you're going to get your nicotine fix. You can either choose the patch or the gum. You should just see how irate new patients get when they hear that they cannot smoke. And believe me, they're no ray of sunshine while they're going through the process of quitting either. I'm sure 99.9% of them just start up again as soon as they get out. The rough part for everyone is that once you're on the floor, that's it. You'll never feel the sun or breathe fresh air again until you get out. However long that may be. Due to the security measures, none of the windows open. You can't feel anything outside. You can't hear anything outside. It does challenge you to not put a smudge on the wishing window. That's for sure. But it wasn't always that way. You used to be able to go outside for about ten minutes (keep in mind prisoners get an hour) once per day to have a cigarette. Being part of this select group was the highest "honor" you could earn on a floor. This selection came down to everything about yourself. Your behavior, the level of your sanity (or insanity), your hygiene, the cleanliness of your room, even your diagnosis. "Smokes!" The staff would yell. I could see all those who were worthy get up, all excited to meet the staff in the main hallway. They would gather there with a nurse and a few guards, and head out. I remember that Mike and Dave would be so excited that even if we were in the middle of a game, they would throw their cards down, jump up, and head to the hallway without even saying a word. We would all put our own cards down and just relax and wait until they returned. We understood the addiction to smoking so we didn't really blame them.

Not only did I not blame them, I envied them! How wonderful it must be to go outside. To feel the sun directly on your skin, to feel the breeze. To just feel the temperature. To hear the leaves, people, cars, and all the other things I could see from the wishing window. How great it must be. Even on a dark and gloomy day, I couldn't hear the rain. I knew they must be able to, because even on a rainy day they still gathered for smokes. I knew they must have some sort of shelter. Finally, one day I had enough of just watching these lucky patients head out off the floor. I gathered the strength and the nerve to request that I be a part of it. When the call for smokes was made, I joined the group in the hallway. I could see the other patients looking at me strangely. Dave whispered to me, half laughing, and asked me what I was doing. But before I could answer him, "You don't smoke Scott." I could hear the nurse say to me. Probably wondering why I was there. "I sure don't ma'am." I replied to the nurse. I made a request to her that I join the smoking group as a way to get outside, even if only for ten minutes, as a way to just get some fresh air. I remember thinking to myself how much I hoped they granted my request. How I hoped they wouldn't send me away from the group looking like a fool. I could see her looking at the guards. The guards looking back at her. Nobody really knowing what to say. The patients themselves even looking confused. Sure, I was another person to keep track of, but I had a very good standing with the guards. Surely they'd know I wouldn't cause any trouble, right? "OK." The nurse simply said as she shrugged her shoulders. Writing my name down on her clipboard. I can't even describe the relief I felt. I couldn't believe it. I was about to go outside!

Dave and Mike smiled big and patted me on the back. Sort of welcoming me to the group, and also happy that my request was granted. And that's how it happened. From then on, even though I was the only one in the group who didn't smoke, I was part of the smoking crew. So, here's how smoking worked. The call for smokes would be made by a nurse. Usually one that had been employed there for a while and was pretty experienced. No matter what we were doing, we'd wait for this call all morning. Excited, we'd jump up and head to meet on the end of the hallway where the hive was. The nurse would be there, as well as two or three guards. We were all told to be quiet as we gathered there because this is when the nurse would write down all of the names of the patients in this lucky group. After all of the names were written down, the nurse would open the smoke locker. This was a tall tan colored metal cabinet. Inside on the top left I could see red and white cartons of Marlboro cigarettes stacked up. These were for the patients who either couldn't afford cigarettes or didn't have any visitors to bring them any. So, they'd actually give them cigarettes! I think it was just easier to give patients smokes than to have to deal with them when they went without them. To the right were stacks of individual packs of cigarettes that belonged to patients who would rather smoke their own brand. Their names were written in black marker on the outside of the pack. First, the nurse would grab the individual packs, read the names on them, and hand them out to the patients. After that, any smoking patient who didn't have their own cigarettes would be handed one by the nurse. Then the nurse would tell us to line up. We'd make a single file line on the right side of the hallway facing away from the hive and looking towards the end of the hall down by the wishing window. The nurse would go to the front of the line along with a guard, while one or two guards would stay at the rear of the line. When everyone was ready and in place, the nurse would start heading towards a door at the end of the hallway. We would not go out the slammer. Remember, you don't cross that med line until you're discharged. They did not want to release us through a doorway that led to the rest of the hospital. We had our own stairway at the opposite end of the hallway that we'd walk down single file to go out to the smoke break. At the bottom of the stairs we exited two doors that led out to a small, concrete structure that greatly resembled a gazebo. Once we were all outside, everyone with their smokes ready, the nurse would take out a lighter from her pocket and hand to a patient. That patient would light their cigarette, and then hand the lighter to another patient, until all cigarettes were lit, and the lighter was given back to the nurse.

Being outside was wonderful. Just as wonderful as I thought it'd be. All the things I could see from the wishing window I could now experience. I could see, hear and smell everything. My senses just fully alive and awake. I remember to the right of me, I had a wide-open view. How great I thought it would be to just run as fast as I could and escape. A silly thought, I very quickly came to realize. I had nothing but the clothes on my back. I had no money. Not even a quarter to use the phone. In addition to those facts, there was also the fact that no escape attempt had ever been successful. I guess I was just so happy to be outside. I leaned back against the wall, tilted my head back, and smiled as a just enjoyed. This was a good time for all of us. Everyone smiled, talked, and were just happy to be outside. Even if it was raining. The only sad part came when it was time to line up single file and go back up to the floor. One floor I was on allowed smoke breaks as well. But I was there during the winter. It was run pretty much the same. We'd gather together, and then head out in a single file line. The doorway in this place went out onto the roof. It was a black tar covered roof that was about twenty feet by thirty feet. You couldn't really see much from it. I remember the dark brown rusted barbed wire that ran about ten feet high all around the perimeter. Anything else you might just be able to climb. But again, we were outside, and we'd savor every minute of it. One night it snowed. We could see it out on the roof in the morning, and we wondered if they would still take us outside for a smoke break. Luckily, they still decided to allow it. As we were going about our march outside, we were very firmly told that there would be no throwing of any snow. I rolled my eyes, thinking how that'd go over like a fart in church. Everybody lit up their smoke first. That was the most important thing. We had to take care of business first. After everyone had their smoke lit, it was probably less than a minute before the first snowball took flight. That's all it took was one. After that, we all picked up the snow. Packing it in our hands and picking out our target. Before we knew it, snowballs were flying everywhere. The staff yelled at us to stop, but did they really think that was going to work? As soon as they raised their voices to us, they found themselves getting pegged as well. What were they going to do? Overpower us all? Take us all one by one to isolation? We hardly thought so. Their only defense was to join in. Smiling all the while, they hurled just as many snowballs at us as we were cucking back at them. I'll never forget that. It was one of the best times I can ever remember on a floor.

The first cigarette I ever smoked came from Dave. Despite the fact that I wasn't of legal age to smoke. I guess it was only a matter of time before I "fully" joined this group. Outside, leaning back against the wall and enjoying the sun and the soft breeze, Dave took a position next to me as he normally would. We'd enjoy being outside and would talk about all kinds of things. One day he said to me, "You've really never smoked?" I told him that I never have. "You can go on and try one if you wanna." He said to me, holding out his pack of cigarettes for me. I admit I did question it in my mind for a moment. On one hand, I didn't really want to be a smoker. On the other hand, look where I am! A smoke would probably cause the least amount of harm to me here. "Sure." I said to Dave. Pulling a long slender cigarette from the rest of them. Dave then asked for the lighter from the nurse and lit my cigarette for me. "There ya go." He said as he handed me my smoke, and took his position back leaning against the wall. I stared down at the lit cigarette, a fine trail of smoke winding off of it. Then I raised it to my lips and took my first drag. I handled it pretty well, I must say. I didn't cough or seem bothered by it at all. But I'll also admit that it did make me a little light-headed. This feeling quickly passed though, and I then leaned against the wall just like Dave and continued to smoke. "You got it now." Dave said, as I continued to smoke, feeling even closer to this group that I've become a part of. I thought to myself that this was pretty nice and relaxing. Especially knowing that in a few minutes I'd be heading back up to our little hell hole. I exhaled the smoke and watched it as it slowly drifted off into the air. "I get it." I thought to myself. I could see how smoking a cigarette would feel good after getting home from a long day at work. Or after any kind of stress or troubling news. After that day, I didn't continue to smoke. I guess having one was more of an experiment, and I did see how it could be enjoyable, but I really just enjoyed being outside. I remember one day, someone walked by and smiled and waved to us. I wondered if they really knew who we were, and why we were there.

Chapter Six: Violence

Violence took place on the floor all the time. I'll give some patients the benefit of the doubt though and say that half of the time there was some sort of reason (usually not reason enough though), and the other half were simply without reason. From my time spent on several different floors over the years, I can tell you that these places are not One Flew Over the Cookoo's Nest, and they're not that horror film you saw that takes place in some old asylum either. They lie somewhere in between. Some sort of violence occurs on floors on a daily basis. It could be patient-on-patient, patient-on-staff, or patient-on-themselves. They also took place during escape attempts too. I think when I look back over the years, that the thing I credit myself with most is not having been in a violent altercation. I absolutely can't believe that I've been in the places that I've been, usually multiple times, and never had to resort to violence. I've come close.

I've come very close. But never quite actually there, and I can't believe it. The only reasons I can imagine for it is that one, usually the patients that became more violent had more severe psychiatric problems, and two, after I had a little more experience on floors, I would usually find myself in a group of four or five friends that stuck together pretty well. You sort of had your "team". I learned rather quickly from my very first stay that forming these relationships would turn out to be very beneficial. Not to mention it just made "doing time" a little better in general. However, you couldn't shake that numbing feeling that, when I look back, is scary to me to this day. The fact that after a while of being on a floor, some sort of fight or violence would break out and you'd hear it and you'd look over your shoulder to see what was going on or who was involved, but then look back at your card game or whatever else you were doing at the time, and simply dismiss it as a normal and regular occurrence that just blurs into the background. In this chapter, I'll discuss some incidents that for some reason stick out to me and I remember better.

      One of the fights that sticks out in my mind took place in the crappiest place I've been in. This is not where I met Dave and the rest of the crew. Although I did go on to meet some people, I was pretty alone at this point. I remember there were two patients. John and Anthony. John was a man of average height. probably in is mid to late twenties. But this was one large country dude. He was a bit shorter, but very stocky and his muscles were huge. I remember his long blonde mullet. He always wore muscle shirts too with no sleeves. His arms were so big. Easily the size of my thighs. I remember his mood too. It's not that he wasn't a nice guy. He was more, tolerant I guess. He was a man of very few words. You could talk to him, ask him a question, and he'd be decent about it. He'd answer or respond to you, but with very few words and almost no change in facial expression. You would kind of just, learn to let him be. Anthony, on the other hand, was quite the opposite. And maybe that would even eventually be the reason for the altercation. He was a tall black male. About the same age as John. Very muscular and fit as well. Again, someone you wouldn't really want to mess with. His personality was a bit different though. He was actually very personable. I can't say he was one of my close friends, but I did have several short discussions with him and he always seemed nice and friendly. However, things were different between him and John. They always sort of snapped at each other. Their remarks to each other were blunt and short. Sometimes I would even go as far to say that they were sizing each other up. Specific examples are hard to give in this case, but the tension was in the atmosphere. Something that's much easier to explain if you see it. I was in the cafeteria of this place one day. It was probably half the size of the place with the wishing window where I met Dave. I wasn't doing much really. Just sitting there and passing time at a small table with a wall to my back, just the way I liked it. John and Anthony later came in and sat down at different tables. I could see them glancing at each other. Shooting each other sort of hateful stares. Eventually words came into play. I honestly can't remember exactly what was said. What I do remember is that I should've left right then. I don't know why I didn't. I actually think I was just bored. So much time on the floor made me want to see a little drama and know how this would unfold. Sure enough, something flat out insulting was said by one of them. I remember John stood up, pushed his chair across the floor, and took a couple of steps towards Anthony in an offensive type manner. Right after this, Anthony did the same thing. Putting the two of them about face to face now. This is now when I finally came to my senses and tried to leave. However, the blows already started to begin. I could see the two of them already shoving and striking each other. Just as I went to run out of the room, not wanting to be caught up in any punishment that came from this, a table from the fight going on slid over and blocked my way out. No shame in running from this, as the staff usually didn't care and just punished everyone there by confining them to their rooms for the rest of the night. Maybe I could've gotten out another way, but at this point, I just decided to get on my knees with my hands on my head. So, there I was. Knees on the floor, hands on my head, and staring directly at the fight between two huge muscular men taking place about five feet in front of me. I just waited too long and had no time to make it out. So, I closely watched the fight as I now had no other option. I could see each fighter land their strikes and hear the smacking sound of fists hitting facial flesh. They carried on as if I was invisible. As if I wasn't even there. Pretty soon drops of blood started to fall and scatter on the floor. Very soon after, the staff in their white coats came. First one, then two, then four in total. The fight was eventually broken up. The two men, their faces splattered with blood, were led out of the cafeteria to their rooms, not to emerge for the rest of the night except to go down to medical one by one for them to briefly check their wounds. There was no iso on this floor. I was told by a guard to stand up. He gripped my hands behind my back and led me to my room. Fortunately, he told me that he knew I was not involved, and that I could emerge from my room in just a few minutes. After about five minutes, I did so, and the night went on as normally as any night does on a floor.

Another somewhat violent incident I remember pretty clearly actually took place during one of the escape attempts I saw. You see, in most facilities, patients usually aren't allowed to just sort of hang out around the med line and main nurse's station without a very good reason to. There are a couple of reasons for that. For one, it just makes the nurses uncomfortable. Of course, attacks have been made against them. Also, the drug den is there, and that's definitely not something you want a patient to have access to. Along with the sharp's locker, which is usually around the same area. One of the most important reasons is because this is as close as a patient comes to the main doors to the floor. If you're hanging around the med line, the nurses will tell you to go to the cafeteria, the hallway, your bedroom, to find any place but there to hang out. Also, even if you do have a reason to be on the line, talking to a nurse about whatever business you have going on, and a staff member comes to the door to request entry or exit, the nurse will tell you to back up about ten feet until the door bolts closed again. Then, you can continue your business. But one time, I saw this precaution ignored. I came out of my room and turned to the right. Walking down the hallway towards the hive. My plan was to request my shaver so that I could trim my facial hair and beard. I was well-liked by the staff at this point, and didn't bother them too much, so usually any questions I had were promptly answered without any issues. The hallway was empty, so right away I noticed Tony up ahead of me waiting by the med line. Just leaning back against the wall. Remember the way I described John previously? Tony was just like him. A big, strong and stocky guy. He had long black hair that he wore in a mullet and didn't really talk to anybody too much. However, he had never previously been violent either. As I approached the line and nurses to ask for my shaver, I assumed Tony was waiting on them as well, and for all I know, he was. I said hello to him and he simply said hello back. What Happened next was the first escape attempt I had ever seen. Just as I was looking towards the nurses and opened my mouth, about to make my request, I heard the buzzing of the main doors and the "thud" of the bolt unlocking them. There was a medical doctor on the other side who wanted in. Before any of us could blink an eye, Tony rushed the doors. He was waiting for this moment. You could tell by how quickly he took off. He didn't even put his hands on the doors. Just as he reached them, he lowered his shoulder into them much like a football player. He hit the doors with immense force. I remember thinking that he could've taken them right off the hinges. The doors swung open so fast, plowing through the doctor and knocking him flat on his back. I could then see Tony quickly run down the hall and out of sight. I could also see the doctor on the floor, trying to get up as blood was running down his nose and chin. The nurses were still behind the desk. I was the one who could reach the doctor first. Out of instinct, I took a step towards the doctor to try to help him. But I very quickly remembered my place. There was nothing I could do but watch the doctor squirm on the floor as the blood ran down his chin and neck. "To your rooms!! To your rooms!!" The nurses shouted as loud as they could. I complied and rushed to my room just as a lot of other patients were doing the same. We remained there for about an hour before we were allowed to come back out. I never saw that doctor or Tony again. I was later told that Tony was captured before he made it out of the hospital.

Self-mutilation was also an issue on just about every floor I've been on. Self-mutilation is done for a few different reasons. One reason is for attention. Due to this fact, and the fact that "cutting" is not very understood to those who don't have experience with mental health, it's unfortunately over-looked and not taken seriously. Another reason is that the person doing this hates themselves for whatever reason and believes that they deserve these wounds and the pain that comes with them. The last reason I'll mention is the most common. Cutting and other forms of self-mutilation usually go hand in hand with depression and anxiety. These conditions are caused by chemical imbalances in the brain. When somebody with this condition cuts or wounds themselves suddenly, the body reacts naturally by releasing dopamine, adrenaline, serotonin, and endorphins into the brain, often leading to a feeling as though these chemical imbalances have been corrected. Of course, there are medications for anxiety and depression that are designed to address these issues by simply swallowing a pill. However, cutting results in a much more immediate and more powerful release of these chemicals. It's hard to imagine, but this provides the person cutting with a very sudden relief, and therefore can actually become addicting. I'll tell you about the worst cutter I've ever seen. He was friends with me, Dave, and a few others who we talked with. His name was Jeff. He didn't normally hang out with us all the time but would here and there. He was a nice and friendly guy. A little "off", but otherwise nice, especially for being a known cutter. But one time he went far beyond the normal small slice. We were all talking in the hallway down by the wishing window. Jeff was there as well. He was talking and laughing at some jokes right along with the rest of us. I could see he kept on playing with a loose piece of metal around a doorway frame. I didn't really think much of it. Maybe I should've. But it seemed to be something he was just sort of absent mindedly doing. Eventually, he broke it off. We could hear the "snap" and see him jolt back a little as it suddenly broke free. We all started laughing, Jeff included. I guess to us it was just comical to break this place, even just a little bit. Jeff looked up at us as we were laughing. He had a big smile on his face, which was red from his own laughter. However, before our smiles even died down, I could see Jeff look down and put an edge of the piece of metal he ripped free against the skin on his forearm. Before I could take one step towards him, he pressed the metal though his skin, and dragged it along the length of his arm towards his wrist and hand. I could see the strength he was putting into this. Then I could see the dark maroon-colored blood follow his movement. All of the sudden, everyone was silent. I was frozen. Some of the rest had their hands over their mouths and faces. Jeff dropped the shard of metal to the floor and looked up at us, actually continuing to smile. Finally, able to move, "Staff!!" I screamed as loud as I possibly could, not knowing what Jeff would do next. At first, I could see the blood drip to the floor, leaving large red circles as it fell.

Then the dripping started to increase until there was more of a steady thin stream. I remember looking at him, then the floor, and then the others. Everything seemed to be slow motion as we dropped to our knees, hearing the staff and guards yelling as they ran down the hall towards us. Our knees hit the floor all at once, as we put our hands over our heads in an attempt to show we had no part in it. We could actually see a look of concern on Jeff's face, before it just became a blank stare. His arm completely red and wet with blood, Jeff was pulled backwards into the arms of staff. The guards stood by us, not knowing yet if this was a self-inflicted wound or not. Staff yelled to each other as Jeff was taken through the slammer and off the floor. We never saw him again. We assumed he was taken somewhere else. We remained on our knees looking at each other. I could see that Dave's face was completely white. A couple of the others were shaking. Either at the sight of the blood, or in fear they'd be blamed for it in some way. Becky was crying. I just looked back at the floor.

Not realizing this sight would remain as a still image in my mind for the rest of time. We were ordered to our rooms. First, we were each questioned separately as to what happened, and then finally all together. But we all had the same story. There are some incidents on the floors that to this day, I feel as though I could reach out and touch the scene if I wanted to. This, without a doubt, is one of them.

Another self-mutilator was Audrey. She was a very nice girl who was about my age. She reminded me a lot of Becky. She was only a harm to herself. Not to anybody else. In fact, I don't remember her ever even speaking rudely to anybody. She was fairly quiet anyway. The poor girl had been in this place for months. She had made improvements I was told, but never quite got well enough to be discharged. Much like the facility where I met Dave and Mike, this one too had a long hallway with patient rooms on either side. There was a large window at the end of this one too. But, it was cloudy type of glass. You couldn't see through it. It was there only to let some light in. There were a couple of comfortable chairs and some plants down by the window. It was a nice place to sit and talk, as this place actually encouraged patients that could do so, to talk to each other about their problems. So, they made a nice private area at the end of the hallway where you could sit and talk. This was actually the nicest place I had ever been in, even though it was actually the farthest from my family. They even separated patients by age. There were three units here. One for children, one for adults (where I was housed), and one for geriatrics. Unfortunately, from what I had been told, the poor children were the worst. You couldn't turn your back on them for a second or they'd attack you. While I was there, one therapist actually got stabbed in the back of the leg by a child with a pencil. However, the food was great here. "Amazing" is probably a better word. You could pretty much get anything you wanted, and as much of it as you wanted. The floors were carpeted, which did wonders for the cold. The bathrooms were large and nice, and even included a shower. Not only that, but you could go outside! There was a large sliding door that went out to a stone patio where staff kept watch. The deal was, you had to stay on the stones. If you didn't, you'd get a warning. If you didn't learn from that, you'd lose your outside privilege. That's how I met Audrey. There were a couple of small tables outside that we'd play Yahtzee on, and she joined in the game. I had a cast on my right hand and wrist when I came to this facility. One day while we were sitting by the window and talking, she asked me what had happened. Although this wasn't the reason I was here, it was because I had punched a wall. It was a dumb-fuck thing to do. Especially with my luck. As it turned out, I hit the wall directly on the 2x4 stud, both breaking and dislocating to of the bones in my hand. I regret telling her this, as it became some sort of challenge against her own self. She had bet that she too could punch a wall hard enough that she would break her hand. You can see now why she wasn't ready to leave yet. She got up and went directly to her room. I followed and stood in the hallway outside of her room, unsure if she was really acting upon this or not. As it turned out, she very much was. She went into her room and stood on her bed facing the cinder block wall. She made a fist with her right hand and made a couple of slow practice taps against the wall. Then, all the sudden, with her eyes narrowed and an angry look on her face, she began to strike the wall with her first as hard as she could. I stood in the hallway wide-eyed and in shock. I didn't want to stop her myself. As a patient, you don't do that, and it was obvious at this time that she could be very unpredictable. Her fist hit the wall about every two seconds. You could clearly hear the smacking sound of her flesh meeting the painted cinder block wall. I could see it almost immediately swell and become purple. Her knuckles were leaving just the smallest amount of blood on the white paint. Now, being a snitch in here isn't like being in prison. Nobody is going to kill you over it.

But, it is very much looked down upon. So, although I thought of alerting the staff, I didn't. This would mean time in isolation for her too. Whatever she would do to herself didn't seem to be life-threatening, so I simply left. The worst case was, she met her goal and broke her hand. Fortunately, she never did.

Tricia was another story. I never quite figured her out. Not completely anyway. I could only go on my guesses about her. Why she was here, what her diagnosis was, what her treats were, etc. Tricia came to this floor after me, but only by a few days. So, she'd basically been there as long as I had been. I could tell this wasn't her first rodeo right off the bat, and also that it might be good to keep her at an arm's length. She was out on the floor no trouble, and her entire demeanor suggested she didn't care about you or anything else that was going on around her. She was a dark person, and no, I don't mean race. She was a white girl, probably a couple of years younger than me. She had a stocky build. Not quite muscular or overweight, but not thin either. She was average height I guess, had shoulder length black hair, dark eyes, fair skin, and always wore black or other dark clothing. Tricia seemed extremely angry. The interesting thing was, you could actually talk to her in passing. You could ask her how she was, if she had visitors today, etc. and she'd actually give a somewhat friendly response. Once in a while she'd actually shoot you a smile. But that smile never left you knowing if she was smiling at you, or even if she knew who you were. Her pupils were as large as a dime the whole time. You see, Tricia had a much different relationship with the guards than the rest of us crazies. This is where her anger comes in. If she had the absolute slightest issue, whether it be with a guard, nurse, or other patient, it was all-out war. Tricia would do the Thorazine shuffle every day. You could count on it. She would scream and holler as the guards carried her off to iso. She would kick against the walls, the floor, all while trying to swing at the guards. She was for sure, the best "dancer" I'd ever seen. When the guards are restraining a patient, they usually try to close the door so that you don't have to witness the event. As if we didn't have enough other shit going on around us on a daily basis. However, it was too hard with Tricia. She just fought too hard. Through the thick and pushed-open wooden door, you could see the guards laying down this fighting girl on the old hospital bed. Then they would struggle to get the thick leather straps around her arms and legs. Once this was done, one of the guards would slam the door shut. Hours later, Tricia would emerge. Her hair all messed up and looking lethargic with those dime-sized pupils. It was one of the strangest things I've seen. Why was she so friendly with the patients, yet horrible with the staff? There were a couple thoughts as to why. It came to the point where some thought that she wanted to fight. That she was addicted to it, or at least enjoyed it enough to take on the guards, day in and day out, leaving the patients alone. Others thought that she simply loved the Thorazine she was given, or maybe that she was addicted to that as well and used her violent behavior as a way to receive it. Either way, seeing Tricia fight, scream, kick, punch, be strapped down with leather belts, and shot full of Thorazine, became such a normal occurrence, that sometimes we didn't even bother to watch. How sad.

Another incident that sticks out to me wasn't violent (as far as I know). But it was the closest escape attempt that I've seen. So I guess I'll just add it to this chapter. It involved two patients. Both were young men who seemed to be about in their late teens or early twenties. I didn't really know them, so I cannot recall their names. They always seemed pretty tight together though. Usually just the two of them would hang out by themselves. I really did get a strange feeling from them. They would sit close together, and also talk close together too. Always as if they didn't want anyone to hear them. You would get this impression that they were always plotting and scheming something. Due to their actions and their escape attempt, I learned something new about the floor. If you looked down the hall towards the wishing window, you'd see the emergency exit on the right side of the hall shortly before the window. The same door that we would exit single file for smokes. The alarm was disarmed by the staff when we left for smokes, and then armed again once we were all gone. As I found out, this was the reason the guards would say "returning" over the radio when we headed back inside. So, they could disarm the alarm to let us back inside. Arming it once again after we had all returned. What I also was unaware of, was that this door automatically unlocks during another situation. This would be during an actual fire, or a fire drill. The fire drills would sound on our floor, but we were never allowed to participate in them. Isn't that smart? Instead, several of us would just gather by the wishing window and look on at all the lucky ones that got to go outside. One morning I could see the two young men hanging out and leaning against the wall down by the emergency door, on the opposite side of the hall. Other than the fact that I noticed that they had been there for a while, I really didn't think much of it. After I had my fill of powder eggs and milk, I decided to spend some time by the wishing window as I often did in the morning. I think over several different stays here, I've actually seen every season through it. The two of them were ten to fifteen feet away from the window, so I didn't think they'd mind. As it turned out, they didn't. As I was looking out the window, doing my morning wishing, the fire alarm suddenly went off. I literally barely had the time to turn my head around before the two men bolted out that door. If you measured the amount of time it took them, you'd be looking at fractions of a second. Including their behavior leading up to this, it was absolutely clear that they were waiting for this. We weren't allowed to participate in fire drills. So, other than going out for smokes, I had never seen this door open before. The only thing I can figure is that at least one of them was near the hive when it was mentioned that there would be a fire drill that morning. Which is why they were just waiting there for it. How they knew that door would disarm and unlock, I don't know. Apparently, they had just done a little more homework than me. On the other hand, I wasn't really interested in escaping. I have to hand it to them. They got farther than anyone else I've seen. What they failed to realize, since they weren't a part of the group that went outside for smokes (or just the fresh air for me), was that there was another door at the bottom of that stairwell that needed to be unlocked by the guards before you could meet the outside world. I had heard that they started bashing the door and severely damaged it, becoming very close to getting outside. However, the guards that chased them down those stairs had caught them in time. It was very close, but still unsuccessful.

Another thing I'll tell you about in this section is not so much violent as it is more disturbing, and is actually an approved treatment called ECT. This stands for electroconvulsive therapy (yes, you read that right). This type of treatment does actually still exist today. It is, however, a little less barbaric then it was in the past. These days, patients receiving this type of therapy are led to a transport van, and then brought to a hospital that conducts it. Once they are there and prepped, they receive anesthetic to knock them out and render them unconscious. After that, several electrodes are placed on their heads. Once everything is all set up, and the doctors are clear, an electric charge is given to the body originating at the head. I'm not exactly sure how high the charge is, but it is enough that once administered, the body will continue to convulse for a period of about sixty seconds. Sounds pretty bad right? It does to me too. However, I'll give the doctors this much. Even though it still isn't fully understood how, it is found to have a positive effect on the psychiatric conditions of 80% of the patients that receive this treatment. On the other hand, it could take up to six months to fully regain your short-term memory. This is why it is only considered for those patients who are not responding well to therapy or medication. I would see these patients return from the hospital to the floor in wheel chairs. They were completely dazed and usually drooling on themselves. They couldn't even remember their own names, let alone yours. They were then taken to their rooms to go to bed. You usually wouldn't see them until the next day, or the day after. One time while I was receiving help voluntarily at an out-patient program, after spending time there in-patient, a couple of doctors took me aside and sat down with me in a meeting room. They had a discussion with me and told me that after they had reviewed my files, they concluded that ECT would be a treatment that they'd like to perform on me. I turned them down and left that day. ECT may be a great option for some people, but it just wasn't for me. I had never considered it as an option.

Remember earlier in the book I mentioned the guy who got stabbed with a fork? I'll go ahead and expand on that one a bit more. These were two guys I didn't know. I was still relatively new to this floor, and hadn't really made a lot of friends yet. This was on the floor that took on a bit more criminals than the others. I was sitting in their crappy little cafeteria. One side of it was completely open to the hallway that led to the patient's rooms on either side. Both men seemed to be about in their mid twenties. They were still in gowns. They either hadn't been here that long, or no matter how long they've been here, hadn't earned their clothes. I'm not sure if these two men knew each other, and if so, what the problem was between the two of them. Or maybe this could have just been a random act of violence, as they do happen. One man was up near the med line here. I could see he was talking to one of the staff members. I couldn't hear what about, and wasn't really trying to. All of the sudden I saw the other man in his gown walking very quickly towards the other one. As of course, you learn to read body language here, I could tell something was wrong. He seemed to be very angry. You didn't even have to had spent time here to figure that out. I assumed his problem was with the staff. Patient's will go off on them for the smallest of reasons. As if this is your vacation home. However, with no warning, he came up behind the other man, pulled a fork from under his gown, and jammed it into the unsuspecting victim's upper back. The victim, after crying out in pain, turned around angrily and faced his attacker. From there it was on, and a hard fight began. This was a facility that required you to go to your bedroom if violence broke out. However, the fight blocked the hallway. So, all we could do was put our hands in the air and watch. You could hear the usual smacking sounds of flesh hitting flesh as the guards jumped on them as fast as they could and broke up the fight. After they broke it up, we were ordered to our rooms. I remember as I walked quickly to my room, I could see a few spots on the wall where blood had splattered. I avoided these men from then on, as they avoided each other. It never was found out how the attacking man was able to get his hands on a metal fork, as this facility (like most) used plastic. Rumor had it that it was packed in some food that a visitor delivered for him. I can only imagine the ass-chewing that staff received for missing that one.

The doctors and staff on the floors will do what they can to help you, and to change you. But, the floors will surely change you as well.

Chapter Seven: Discharge

So, after an ambulance, police car, or family member has brought you here, how do you get out? Well I'll tell you one simple way. It doesn't do much to help you with whatever problems you have, but it is effective when it comes to being released from this place you've been committed to. You see, whenever you are committed, you have the legal right to a 72-hour release hearing. By law, once you request the paperwork for this, the staff must provide it to you. You simply fill out this paperwork and return it to the staff. Once it is submitted to the staff, the facility has 72 hours to put you in a court where a judge will make a final ruling as to whether or not you're a threat to yourself or others. I imagine that with most patients, it's a pretty clear-cut case. But if you compose yourself well and are smart about how you complete the paperwork, it could be a different story. The best time to submit your completed forms is on a

Thursday or Friday. The reason being, it will take the staff a little bit of time to submit these forms. Also, it's rare that a judge will see you on a Saturday or Sunday. I've only attempted this twice, when both times I really didn't believe I needed to be on a floor. Both times I exercised my right to have a 72-hour release hearing was on a Thursday, and I was discharged the next day. The best way to be discharged is through your conduct and participation during therapy. On most floors there are therapy sessions two or three times a day. Some patients don't participate. It's either just too soon for them, or they just don't care. But even though they can't make you, it's always stressed by the staff that you participate. It's always the same type of thing you'd imagine or have seen on TV. A bunch of us sit in a circle with a therapist present. It's pretty awkward at first. There are a lot of other patients there, you don't know them, and are definitely concerned about what they think of you. You may not even be ready to come fully out with your problems anyway. But the fact of the matter is that, you will sit down with the head psychiatrist of the floor once a week. There is a weekly visit with this man or woman who determines your fate. This doctor will look at a few different things. One is your behavior and demeanor. Another is your behavior during your stay. Have you been angry? Have you lashed out? Do you get along well with others? Is your hygiene good? Have you responded to medication? Finally, what do the therapist's notes say about you? That last one is the most important of all. Waiting to see the doctor is the most anxiety producing thing of all. You will sit before his or her desk, watch them flip through pages in your file, and just wait for them to say anything at all. As they analyze your progress, they will ask you some simple questions. How are you feeling? How have therapy groups been for you? How do you feel on your current medications? Then, if you've been here long enough, stayed out of trouble, and you've shown enough progress as far as your mental state, you will hear those magical words. "Well, our current plan is to discharge you tomorrow." There's no holding back the excitement when you here this. Your eyes widen, the biggest smile comes to your face, and you can't help but cry out "Yes!", and say thank you about a million times. As we all waited upon the doctor, you could tell who was decided to be released just by the look on their face. The same look and excitement I'm sure I've had many times. So now you know that you will be discharged the next day. What do you do now? The first thing you do is inform others. Unable to keep this exciting news to yourself. Since the doctors are very hard to read, the patients are just as excited and surprised as you are. Directly following that, you would approach the hive and request that the staff call whoever it is that will be transporting you from the facility and let them know of your discharge date and time. This was a wonderful feeling. Since someone else (usually my mother) knew of your discharge, it made it even that much more real, and they're always excited about your release. That night you were the happiest person there. Everybody would ask you where you were going, what your plans were etc. All in envy that you knew for sure that you were getting out. Then, after a sleepless night in bed, the next morning would come. You would be so giddy. The staff would give you several large plastic bags. With these, you would put all of your clothes in, and any other personal things you wanted to take with you. Then they'd take you to the sharp's locker. Here, you take anything you checked in during your time on this floor, along with any other property you had on you when you were committed. I have to admit, there was also a bit of anxiety when leaving the floor. You knew that from here, you have to take on going back to school, your job, living alone and taking care of your home if that were the case, but you had to trust the doctors and your discharge plan that you were ready. You'd have to trust yourself that you were ready. So then, it came time. You were ready to go, and the staff has told you that your ride is on the way. I always remember giving my room one final lookover before I left. Not just to make sure that I packed all of my belongings, but to also say goodbye. Then I would say goodbye to my friends. This was the one time when hugs were understood and permitted. After that, holding my bags in my hands, I would take the most important steps you ever take one a floor. While your ride was on their way, you were permitted to cross the med line and wait by the main doors. To be completely honest, this was very exciting and very strange at the same time. During your entire stay, this was strictly forbidden. However, now I would walk to the med line, look down at my feet, and just watch them as they crossed over the thick red line on the floor. I was permitted to wait by the slammer until my ride arrived. My friends would stand at the other side of the med line and look on as another patient got to walk out those doors. It was so strange to stand and wait on this side of the line and look back at them. Usually it was my mother that came to get me. God bless her. Everyone, sometimes even including staff, would smile and wave goodbye as we left.

It's always amazing leaving the floor. You've even forgotten about the outside world for so long. I could smell the fresh air and look back at the hospital knowing that I don't have to go back inside. I'm not really sure why, but I always loved being in a moving car while I was leaving. It was always my favorite thing. I think I was just happy to be heading away from that place. Also, I could see everything pass by me right up close. Just as I had seen it from the wishing window. The streets, houses, other cars, people, and all these things that I've been kept so far away from. It's sort of hard to explain, but it all looked so much clearer too. So much more vivid. There was no more looking at things through thick glass and wire. I remember getting home too. How wonderful it was to take a nice hot shower. A full-size shower, no time limit, and no guard standing outside the door ready to shut it down. Food was great as well. I could eat as much of it as I wanted to. Pizza was my favorite. It was either homemade, ordered, or my mother would cook me one of my favorite home-cooked meals. Sometimes my father would make me a hot meatball sub. He's Italian, so his cooking was always great too. But either way, it was big, hot, and real food. It tasted so good. Driving my own car was great as well. I could get in it and just cruise. I think it was more symbolic than anything. I had the freedom to go wherever I want, as far as I want and as fast as I want. It was nice to be in control of these things. You had the joy of looking forward to these things every time you stepped back across the med line. There were a couple of things that were difficult for me when I got out. One was that I needed some sort of light in my bedroom at night. Have you ever stayed at a hotel and woken up in the middle of the night thinking that you were home in bed? The same thing would happen after I was released from a floor. When I woke up at night, I needed to know immediately that I was at home in my own bed and not locked away anymore. Sometimes I would dream that I was still there. I still have some dreams here and there even to this day. Which is why I still sleep with some sort of dim light at night. Even if it's just what comes from my alarm clock. The other thing that was difficult for me then, and still makes me uncomfortable today, was having people behind my back who I cannot see. In a line or a crowd, I find myself often looking over my shoulder to keep an eye on things. Or if I go to a restaurant and am seated by a hostess, I will choose the seat at that table that faces the most people, and have my back to less people. I haven't really told many people about this, and I'm not sure if they've noticed. But it's a couple of things that my time spent on the floors has ruined for me. Like I said, for better or for worse, they will change you.

Epilogue

I'm still on the road I've been on all of my life, because we don't get another one. But we can go fast, slow, curve and turn. It can be bumpy or smooth. We can go through rain and storms, and we can go through clear beautiful sunshine. To me, there is no "road less traveled", or one that could've taken you in a different direction. You only get one, and hope you have the strength to see the end. I'm in the middle of my road now. But in my rear-view mirror, should I choose to look at it, I see a lot of darkness. While the road ahead, where my focus is, even if it has some bumps in it, looks much brighter. I'm currently 38 years old, and honestly, I'm living my dream. My dream during all those hard times was to just be a normal guy. How I envied other people who were. I'll never be completely out of the woods as far as my mental health, but I have made leaps and bounds over the last decade, and am probably about as good as I'm going to get. It took a long time to find the right doctor for me. As well as the right medications and doses. But I never thought I'd even be here. I didn't know if I had the strength it takes. I see my psychiatrist (the best in the business) about every six weeks. I believe that's still very healthy and important to me. I have been stable on the same medications for the past 13 years. But I also have my dream. A wife, house, kid. All of the things I never dreamed I'd ever have. I haven't seen the inside of a psychiatric facility in 13 years, and don't believe that I ever will again. I must say, that I don't regret all these times spent in these facilities. I saw a whole lot beginning at a young age, but I don't see it as a wasted youth. I believe all of the experiences you went through in the past help shape who you are today. I can say that I've had a hard time. But I believe that today, I am a stronger person. I appreciate what I have even more. I'm simple. I don't fear much, and I don't want for much. And, I do not envy other people the way I used to. I do honestly feel somewhat hardened. Even if only a little. I'm not as bothered, disturbed or phased by things as much as the average person would be. I do apologize to my family and friends for any trouble I've caused them over the years, but thank them so much for sticking with me. I literally owe my life to them. I also have plans for the future. They may not seem all that big to you, but they are huge to me. My plans are to continue to be a loving husband and father. To sit on the beach during family vacations, never forgetting where I came from. To keep loving seeing all of my family members, and bringing a smile to my little nieces and nephews faces. I do have advice for you, the reader. If you know someone who has mental illness, try not to keep the stigma that surrounds it alive. Many of us are just like anybody else trying their best to overcome a serious medical issue. Be kind, and if you do feel that you need to, don't be afraid to take action if you think they need serious professional help. You may just save a life. If you are a person reading this who has mental illness, let this be your proof that life can be better. No matter what your diagnosis is (I've had a few over the years). I spent a whole lot of time fighting these hardships. But would I go through that in order to have the entire rest of my life? Absolutely. There is no doubt in my mind that it was worth it. Do not be afraid to admit your problems and seek help. I came so close to missing out on this life. Gather your strength, close your eyes, and tell yourself what I have told myself many times....

Just keep breathing.

"Long is the way, and hard, that out of hell leads up to light." – Paradise Lost